Mr. Pei's Perfect SHAPES

THE STORY OF ARCHITECT I. M. PEI

Written by **Julie Leung**   Illustrated by **Yifan Wu**

Quill Tree Books
An Imprint of HarperCollinsPublishers

Little Ioeh Ming Pei grew up spending his summers in Suzhou with his grandfather.

Together they strolled the city's famous gardens, where volcanic rocks loomed like statues.

One day, his grandfather asked, "Do you know how the rock came to look this way?"

Ioeh Ming shook his head.

"A rock farmer took this rock, chiseled small holes into it, and 'planted' it in a stream.

"The fast-moving water widened the holes and smoothed down the edges over many, many years.

"The farmer could only imagine how the rock would change.
Only his grandchildren will see the final shape."

Ioeh Ming studied the curves of the stone.
What careful planning it must take to design such
masterpieces for future people to enjoy!

In 1927, when Ioeh Ming was ten years old, his father moved the family to Shanghai.

The city boomed and bustled with business.

Everywhere Ieoh Ming Pei looked, buildings were going up.

源茂盛 织
缎
绸 棉 呢
缎 布 羢

嘉福綢緞局

眼鏡

中秋

五
芳
懋
各色大麯 经源客饭随意

件袱桂

煙紙园各

Every weekend, Ieoh Ming would pass the
construction site for the glamorous Park Hotel, rising
like a mountain on Nanjing Road.
   He sketched the building as the walls rose higher
and higher until it reached twenty-two floors.
   The tallest Ioeh Ming had ever seen!

Such a building was sure to last many lifetimes, he thought.

He imagined what it might be like to design something just as grand and enduring.

When Ieoh Ming turned eighteen, he traveled to America to study architecture—the design and construction of buildings. For much of the previous century, buildings were modeled after older, traditional designs:

Grecian columns and Gothic arches.
Dramatic statues and decorative accents.
Some buildings looked more like cakes.
But a new way of thinking was becoming popular: modernism.

Out with the old, Ioeh Ming's teachers said, and in with the new.
Modernism was all about simple geometric shapes and clean lines
and using new materials such as steel, glass, and concrete.

At school, Ioeh Ming was determined to make a name for himself. In fact, he even shortened his name to I.M. so that Americans would have an easier time pronouncing it.

Meanwhile, he met Eileen Woo, another Chinese student
studying in America.

They fell in love, married, and began a family.

After World War II, I.M. and Eileen wanted to move back to China.

But when the country fell under Communist rule and cut off ties
with the world, I.M. realized there would be no future for him there.

I.M. became an American citizen and worked as an architect in New York City, designing public housing and low-cost skyscrapers.

Throughout the 1950s, everywhere I. M. Pei looked, his buildings were going up.

But I.M. wanted to be known for more than just high-rises and housing.

He did not forget the lessons from the beautiful rocks in Suzhou.

He wanted to shape something that would be admired for generations.

After President John F. Kennedy was assassinated in 1963, architects everywhere wondered who would get the job of designing the presidential library in his honor.

Kennedy's widow, Jackie, interviewed all the notable architects of the time, including the up-and-coming I. M. Pei. It was Pei, with his forward-thinking tastes, who reminded Jackie most of her late husband's spirit.

By winning the project, I. M. Pei became famous overnight. Suddenly, museums, companies, banks, and even governments all wanted an I. M. Pei creation.

For each project, I.M. thought deeply about how a well-designed building stood in harmony with the environment around it.

The shape of it should not only look beautiful but improve people's lives.

In 1985, the Bank of China hired I. M. Pei to build Asia's tallest tower in Hong Kong.

He puzzled over how the building could meet their high expectations and still withstand the city's powerful typhoons.

The higher the skyscraper, the more steel is needed for the stabilizing columns at the building's center.

But I.M. only had a tiny plot of land to work with and seventy-two floors to build.

Instead, he was inspired to use diagonal braces to crisscross the face of the building in diamond shapes and distribute the weight to the four corners.

I.M.'s thinking opened up the possibility of even taller buildings in the future.
He invented a whole new way to build skyscrapers.

When I. M. Pei was tasked with adding a modern wing to the National Gallery of Art in Washington, DC, the only land available was an awkward, uneven trapezoid.

On a flight back to New York, I. M. Pei doodled the trapezoid over and over.

In one sketch, he drew a diagonal slash through the form, simply splitting it into two triangles nestled next to each other.

I. M. Pei smiled. He had found the perfect shape.

When the modern wing was finally revealed, art critics and fellow architects were amazed by the beautiful, simple symmetry of the two buildings and how they lined up perfectly with the original museum's entrance.

I. M. Pei's most well-known shape, however, was for the most famous art museum in the world—the Louvre in Paris.

At the time, the old building had fallen into disrepair. The president of France hired I. M. Pei to fix it up.

I.M. made several trips to study the Louvre in secret. He saw for himself how its U-shaped hallways confused visitors and how there was no easy way to go from one end of the museum to the other.

I.M. decided on a central, *underground* entrance to be placed in the center of the U.

And above it?

A towering seventy-one-foot vaulted glass pyramid.

When I. M. Pei's plans debuted, Parisians hated the idea. There were angry words hurled at I.M. in public. Many questioned why a Chinese American and not a French architect had been awarded the job.

But I. M. Pei knew when he had found the perfect shape.

"Just wait," he said repeatedly. "Time will tell."
When the scaffolding finally came down, the glass
pyramid gleamed like a sparkling jewel, reflecting the
beauty of the existing building around it.

Visitors could now navigate the vast museum more easily.
These days, I. M. Pei's pyramid is celebrated as an icon of Paris.

In nearly every part of the
world, an I. M. Pei building
has gone up:

From the craggy peaks of the Rocky Mountains

to the arid desert city of Doha.

From mad-scramble metropolitan Hong Kong

to a serene, remote Japanese forest.

Each carefully planned
by a man who could foresee how the
shape of a building must harmonize with nature,
with people, and with time.

Late in his life, the city of Suzhou approached I. M. Pei to design a museum for the region's art.

Honoring traditional Chinese architecture, I.M. used white-washed plaster walls and gray clay roof tiles throughout the building.

He also incorporated the modern shapes that had made
him famous: sharp patterns of triangles and quadrangles and
light-filled atriums of glass.
An ode to the past and a tribute to the future.

At nearly ninety years old, I.M. returned
to the gardens he used to visit as a
boy, this time to install a masterpiece of his
own making, just like the rock farmers of
his childhood who imagined perfect shapes
for their grandchildren to see.

Timeline

April 26, 1917	Ioeh Ming Pei is born in Guangzhou, China.
1927	When I.M. is ten years old, his father relocates the family to Shanghai, China.
1935	Moves to the United States to study architecture at the University of Pennsylvania
1942	Marries Eileen Woo
1948	Begins his first job out of graduate school with William Zeckendorf, designing mostly high-rise buildings
1949	I.M.'s first building is completed—a simple two-story corporate building for Gulf Oil in Atlanta, Georgia.
1964	Is selected as the architect for the John F. Kennedy Presidential Library and Museum
1978	The East Building of the National Gallery of Art in Washington, DC, is completed.
1979	The John F. Kennedy Presidential Library and Museum in Boston, Massachusetts, is completed.
1989	The Louvre Pyramid in Paris, France, is completed. The Bank of China Tower in Hong Kong, China, is completed.
1995	The Rock & Roll Hall of Fame in Cleveland, Ohio, is completed.
2006	The Suzhou Museum in Suzhou, China, is completed.
2008	The Museum of Islamic Art in Doha, Qatar, is completed.
May 16, 2019	I.M. dies in New York City at the age of 102.

Selected Sources

Books

Cannell, Michael T. *I. M. Pei: Mandarin of Modernism*. New York: Random House, 1995.

Rubalcaba, Jill. *I. M. Pei: Architect of Time, Place, and Purpose*. Tarrytown, NY: Marshall Cavendish, 2011.

Documentaries

Lacy, Susan, creator. *American Masters*. Season 24, episode 2, "I. M. Pei: Building China Modern." Aired March 31, 2010, on PBS.

Landin, Bo, and Sterling Van Wagenen, dirs. *Learning from Light: The Vision of I.M. Pei*. Slickrock Films, 2009.

Rosen, Peter, dir. *First Person Singular: I.M. Pei*. Peter Rosen Productions, 1997.

For Wendi, and all we've built
—J.L.

For my mother and my grandmothers
—Y.W.

Quill Tree Books is an imprint of HarperCollins Publishers.

Mr. Pei's Perfect Shapes: The Story of Architect I. M. Pei
Text copyright © 2024 by Julie Leung   Illustrations copyright © 2024 by Yifan Wu
All rights reserved. Manufactured in Italy.
No part of this book may be used or reproduced in any manner whatsoever without written permission
except in the case of brief quotations embodied in critical articles and reviews. For information address
HarperCollins Children's Books, a division of HarperCollins Publishers, 195 Broadway, New York, NY 10007.
www.harpercollinschildrens.com
Library of Congress Control Number: 2023944100
ISBN 978-0-06-300630-0
The artist used her hand-drawn method with love to create the digital illustrations for this book.
Typography by Rachel Zegar   24 25 26 27 28 RTLO 10 9 8 7 6 5 4 3 2 1   First Edition